T0400620

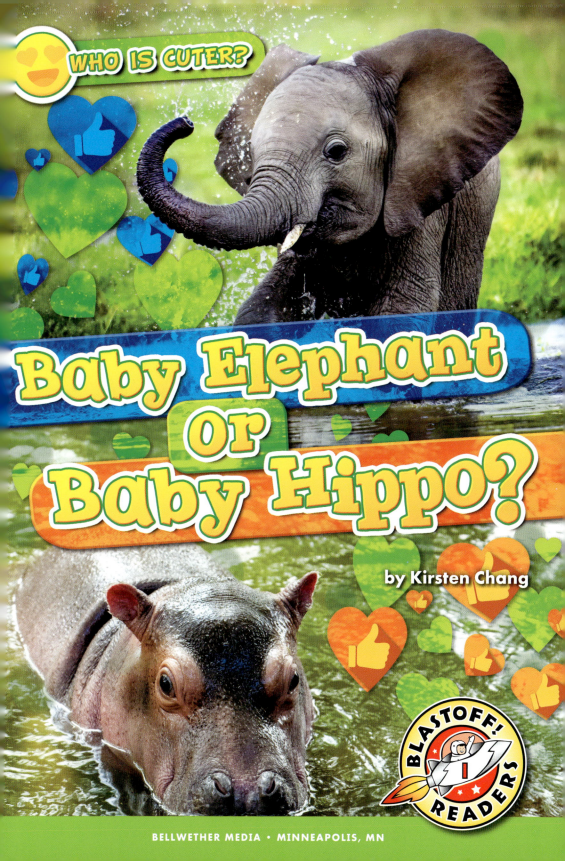

Baby Elephant Or Baby Hippo?

by Kirsten Chang

BELLWETHER MEDIA • MINNEAPOLIS, MN

BLASTOFF! READERS

Blastoff! Readers are carefully developed by literacy experts to build reading stamina and move students toward fluency by combining standards-based content with developmentally appropriate text.

Level 1 provides the most support through repetition of high-frequency words, light text, predictable sentence patterns, and strong visual support.

Level 2 offers early readers a bit more challenge through varied sentences, increased text load, and text-supportive special features.

Level 3 advances early-fluent readers toward fluency through increased text load, less reliance on photos, advancing concepts, longer sentences, and more complex special features.

★ **Blastoff! Universe**

Reading Level

Grade **K**

Grades **1–3**

Grade **4**

This edition first published in 2026 by Bellwether Media, Inc.

No part of this publication may be reproduced in whole or in part without written permission of the publisher. For information regarding permission, write to Bellwether Media, Inc., Attention: Permissions Department, 6012 Blue Circle Drive, Minnetonka, MN 55343.

Library of Congress Cataloging-in-Publication Data

LC record for Baby Elephant or Baby Hippo? available at: https://lccn.loc.gov/2025003207

Editor: Rachael Barnes   Designer: Brittany McIntosh

Printed in the United States of America, North Mankato, MN.

Table of Contents

Cute Calves

Baby elephants and baby hippos are big! They are both called calves.

elephant
calf

hippo
calf

5

Both **mammals** stay close to their moms. They drink her milk.

Ears and Noses

Elephant calves have big ears that flap.
Hippo calves have small ears.
They wiggle!

Elephant calves have long **trunks** for noses.
Hippo calves have round **snouts**.

trunk

round snout

Elephant calves have wrinkly skin. Hippo calves have smooth skin.

Elephant calves
live on land.
Hippo calves spend
more time in water.

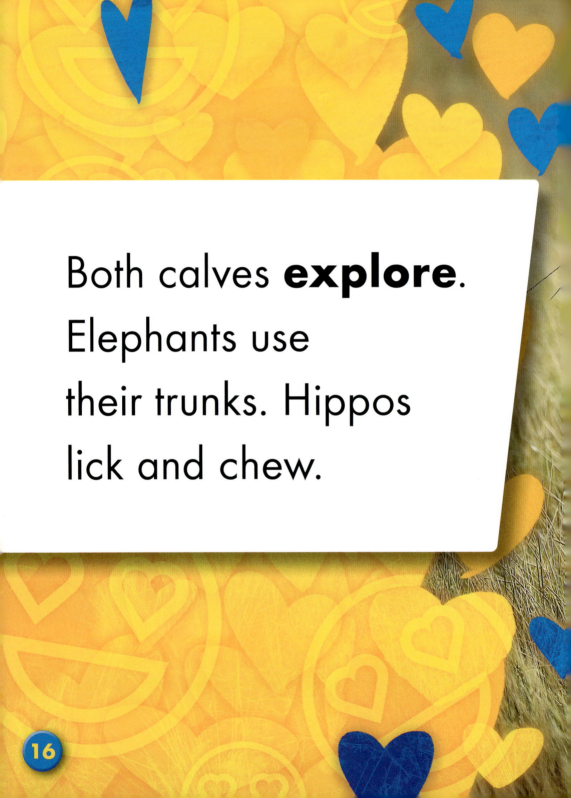

Both calves **explore**.
Elephants use
their trunks. Hippos
lick and chew.

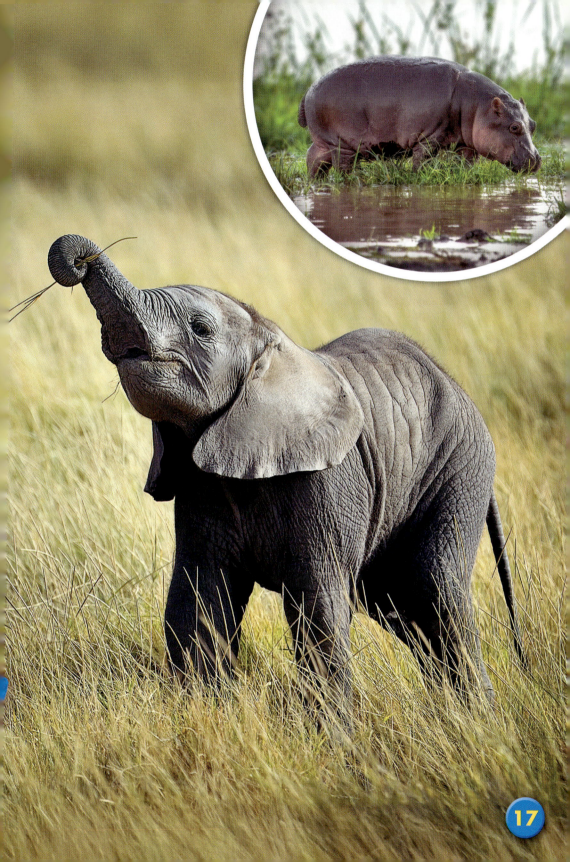

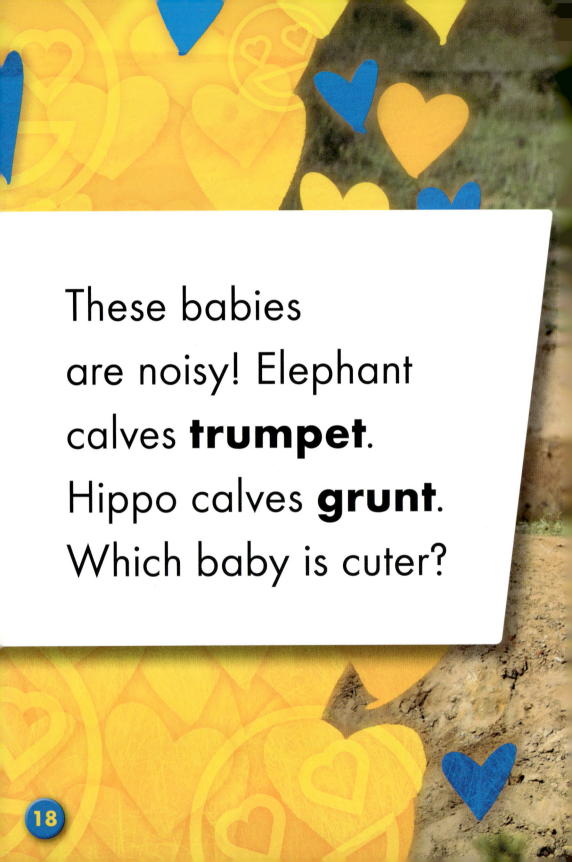

These babies
are noisy! Elephant
calves **trumpet**.
Hippo calves **grunt**.
Which baby is cuter?

trumpeting

grunting

Who Is Cuter? 😍

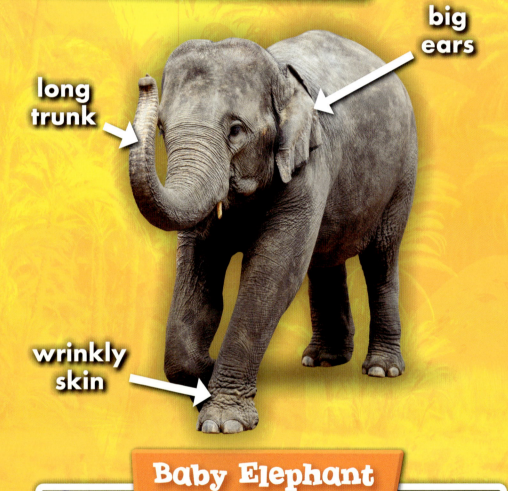

big
ears

long
trunk

wrinkly
skin

Baby Elephant

lives
on land

explores
with its
trunk

trumpets

small
ears

Who is your pick?
Vote at
BellwetherMedia.com

round
snout

smooth
skin

Baby Hippo

spends
more time
in water

licks and
chews to
explore

grunts

21

Glossary

explore

to walk and look around to learn about a new place

snouts

the noses and mouths of some animals

grunt

a short, low sound

trumpet

to make a horn sound with a trunk

mammals

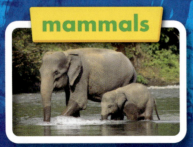

warm-blooded animals that have backbones and feed their young milk

trunks

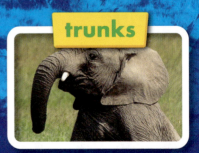

the long noses and upper lips of some animals

To Learn More

AT THE LIBRARY

Barnes, Rachael. *Baby Hippos*. Minneapolis, Minn.: Bellwether Media, 2023.

Brandle, Marie. *Elephant Calves in the Wild*. Minneapolis, Minn.: Jump!, 2023.

Rathburn, Betsy. *Baby Elephants*. Minneapolis, Minn.: Bellwether Media, 2024.

ON THE WEB

FACTSURFER

Factsurfer.com gives you a safe, fun way to find more information.

1. Go to www.factsurfer.com.

2. Enter "baby elephant or baby hippo" into the search box and click 🔍.

3. Select your book cover to see a list of related content.

Index

The images in this book are reproduced through the courtesy of: Romi Gamit, front cover (elephant); odd-add, front cover (hippo); Andre Klopper, p. 3 (top); Eric Isselee, pp. 3 (bottom), 21 (top); Mari Swanepoel, p. 5 (elephant); Nature Picture Library/ Alamy, p. 5 (hippo); GomezDavid, p. 6 (elephant); Jake Lyell/ Alamy, p. 6 (hippo); Linda Smit Wildlife Impressions/ Alamy, p. 8 (hippo); David Noton Photography/ Alamy, p. 8 (elephant); Dawie Nolte, p. 11 (elephant); robertharding/ Alamy, p. 11 (hippo); Tikling, p. 13 (hippo); Stephaniellen, p. 13 (elephant); Johann Marais, p. 15 (elephant); Little Things Abroad, p. 15 (hippo); Satheesh Rajh Rajagopalan/ Alamy, p. 17 (hippo); Diana Robinson Photography/ Getty Images, p. 17 (elephant); Friedrich von Hörsten/ Alamy, p. 19 (elephant); Sherry Epley, p. 19 (hippo); Boonrod, p. 20 (top); Pascale Gueret, p. 20 (bottom left); SD photography, p. 20 (bottom center); MFadly29, p. 20 (bottom right); AfriPics.com/ Alamy, p. 21 (bottom left); jtstewartphoto, p. 21 (bottom center); FotoRequest, p. 21 (bottom right); CK-TravelPhotos, p. 22 (explore); i viewfinder, p. 22 (grunt); jufrisphtr, p. 22 (mammals); ylq, p. 22 (snouts); Francois van Heerden, p. 22 (trumpet); Chedko, p. 22 (trunks).